A CHILD'S VOYAGE TO NEW LIFE

A CHILD'S VOYAGE TO NEW LIFE

Memoir of a Little Italian Girl

Rose Catalano

A CHILD'S VOYAGE TO NEW LIFE
MEMOIR OF A LITTLE ITALIAN GIRL

iUniverse books may be ordered through booksellers or by contacting:

iUniverse
1663 Liberty Drive
Bloomington, IN 47403
www.iuniverse.com
1-800-Authors (1-800-288-4677)

ISBN: 978-1-5320-1186-3 (sc)
ISBN: 978-1-5320-1187-0 (hc)
ISBN: 978-1-5320-1188-7 (e)

Print information available on the last page.

iUniverse rev. date: 11/21/2016

Testimonials

Having enjoyed *This Head of Security Wears High Heels*, I look forward to reading Rose's next book. For the last twenty years, I've had the privilege of watching her successfully grow her business and courageously face whatever challenges were thrown her way. It is because of determined entrepreneurs like Rose that immigrants and children of immigrants have been labeled the engine of growth that allows Canada to prosper.

—John Scura, chartered accountant

Being well aware of Rose's level of professional knowledge and having read her previous book, *This Head of Security Wears High Heels*, I believe this new book enables and inspires one and all to be the best we can be. It truly is an ought-to-read manuscript.

—Ann Silar, senior editor, *Women of Distinction* magazine

I thoroughly enjoyed reading Rose's first book, *This Head of Security Wears High Heels*. Her story is very real, practical and strategic. The presentation was so well structured that it made the book a non-stop read. This book also commands my attention.

—Marlon Ruiz, project supervisor

Rose brings intelligence, charm and integrity in challenging stereotype organizations/cultures. She has proven to competently engage in, and achieve excellence in, a male-dominated profession. I look forward to her new book, which I anticipate will be equally as rewarding and informative as her first book.

—Susan Aiken, CMA/CPA

Dedication

This book is dedicated to my grandmother (*nonna*) Maria Rosa, a woman whose actions spoke volumes and whose spirit was of immeasurable worth. She taught me to live my life with meaning and to believe in my individualism and my potential to make solid and spontaneous decisions. She also encouraged tackling a challenge head-on and acting according to its merits.

Her philosophy was this: *It is better to act on a given situation and risk being wrong than to do nothing about it at all.* She believed that "yes, there is another way" is more significant than "no, there is no other way."

Acknowledgments

My first thank you goes to my family for their continued support through the long hours I spent recollecting and documenting details of my childhood experiences and the memories of my journey to Canada. Without their untiring zeal to bring this story to light, I might not have succeeded in getting this book to the publishing stage. To them, I say thank you, and I know that I will always hold your enthusiasm dear and deep in my heart.

I also extend my unreserved appreciation to my editor, Ann Jordan-Mills. Ann, your expertise has been my true guide all the way from the beginning to the end of this book's journey. Thank you.

I am grateful to my friends and colleagues who have shared and debated with me many thoughts and theories regarding immigration standards and policies, business endeavours, economic accomplishments and the value of positive thinking. After all, being negative takes as much or more energy as being positive, so why waste good energy to make things gloomy?

Thank you, and let's keep talking.

Foreword

I was very pleased when Rose asked me to edit her manuscript, having worked very closely with her on her first book. When I began to read, however, my feeling turned to delight. Her words brought back so many memories of the time when I myself sailed to Canada many years ago as a young married woman.

Our respective parents drove us to the Liverpool docks, and our families were allowed onto the ship, the Carinthia, to settle us in and say goodbye. At that time, in the late sixties, we didn't really know when we might see each other again, because transatlantic air travel was in its infancy, and we were the first of all our siblings to leave England. Everyone was sad, but at the same time they were rejoicing for us in our new life adventure. I remember my mother remarking at the wisdom of my mother-in-law to bring her sunglasses-the better to hide her tears!

Like Rose, I remember the Dining Room on our ship-not so much for the food, but for the attendance at meals-or rather, the lack of. It was packed for dinner the first night and, once we go out into the open sea on the second night, it was almost empty. We were placed at a table of about ten people, and both of us being rather shy (then), we didn't at first speak up about the fact that we were a couple, so we ended up sitting at opposite ends of the table with no-one else to talk to. That was remedied when the seats opened up once the sea-sickness hit most people-including me, after a couple of days. I visited the medical centre and was given a shot, which helped enormously, and I was back on my feet shortly, with a dining seat next to my husband.

I really don't remember a whole lot about those days in between leaving Liverpool and arriving in Halifax, Nova Scotia, save that there was constant creaking of the ship's timbers in the rough January weather on the Atlantic, and a whole lot of water surrounding us. That voyage seemed unending, and I don't particularly have any memories that stand out, though I do recall meeting a few other young couples. I do, however, remember what happened when we disembarked at what is now known as Pier 21.

Our crates and boxes were unloaded and we all had to stand beside our belongings while the Customs Officials did their thing. They appeared stern-they had to be, I suppose! But it was the picture of what I observed happening to people lined up next to us from another ship that I have always kept in my mind and heart.

These men were literally ransacking their crates and trunks, obviously looking for contraband such as meats and other food. They used crowbars to wrench open the wooden crates-breaking them apart in the process - with clothes and other belongings spilling out onto the concrete. I remember seeing them holding high large thick sausages, the kind that you might see in a deli on a meat slicer. It was almost as if they were trophies, and their smiles were of triumph that they had found what they were looking for.

Now I know that those items are not allowed, and I accept that. However, the items represented the comforts of a home these people had left far behind. Surely there could have been more humane ways of removing them and even explaining the reasons why the meats should not have been brought to Canada in the first place. In my memory, the removal of the meat was not really the worst thing; it was the blatant disrespect, you could almost call it abuse, in the way it was done. And I have forever felt sad for those immigrants and wondered how their crates and boxes were repaired and re-packed for the onward journey.

From the Customs Hall, we were directed onto a train which was waiting for us there in the dark. It was January and, having left the ocean, we now spent several days traveling through what seemed like another sea-this time of white. I recall passing close to many pretty little towns. They were small and sleepy, with the streets looking empty of inhabitants and instead covered in snow. I had left behind a green England, and arrived in a white Canada, via a grey and angry ocean.

Our train was the old Canadian Pacific (CP), which arrived in Edmonton, Alberta, 18 hours late at 5:30 in the morning, so my life in Canada was officially beginning.

But this is Rose's story, not mine …

Ann Jordan-Mills

Introduction

Is Canada my home now? Could this be the beginning of a colourful adventure that I will write about one day when I am old enough to tell my story?

There was no point in pretending I knew what all the commotion in our house in Italy was about, nor was I privy to my parents' real plans. It all seemed like a masquerade that kept the hearts of both the young and the mature thumping at an accelerated rhythm. I observed a number of strange events slowly unfolding as I struggled to grasp the real purpose of this chaos. It was hard for me to feign excitement or bask in fanciful thoughts when, without prior warning that April evening, my two siblings and I were dressed for travel and told not to stray from our assigned spot. A cab would arrive momentarily to transport all five of us to the seaport in Naples.

But why? I had so many questions, and no one was willing to answer any of them. I was simply told that we were leaving our home behind to travel far and relocate to a New World.

Well, what does that mean to a young child who is not familiar with such geographical details? Did it mean we were embarking on a lifestyle of drifters? Where was this New World, and why were we going there? The questions kept pounding in my head all through the night. As the morning dawned, I became even more disoriented as I saw so many strangers joining us on that Neapolitan dock, but no other family members. I asked myself, *Does the New World only have room for these strangers, my parents, myself and my two brothers?* If that was the case, then I wanted to be straightforward and tell my parents that I rejected their plan and that my siblings most assuredly did too.

As the hours ticked away, my parents did their best to keep things moving, and before the day ended, we boarded an enormously imposing ship: the *Vulcania*. We were on our way to Halifax, Nova Scotia—the New World.

I had another question: Why did everyone seem so blasé about this trip?

Time seemed to be frozen for us until that ear-splitting foghorn signalled that we were on our way across the Atlantic Ocean. We would be at sea all the way to Canada—ten days, port-to-port. But reaching Nova Scotia was not all this journey entailed for us. From there, we had to continue on to our final destination: Toronto, Ontario. It was a good thing I did not have red hair, otherwise the colour of my face would have matched my hair once I realized that was the case.

The trip from Nova Scotia to Toronto took two days, and then finally it was time to rejoice, as we reunited with my father's younger brother and his family who had immigrated to Canada a few years prior. Of course, by now, they were to some extent acclimatized to this new land. Different languages, new school systems, unusual (to us) residential dwellings, many new means of transportation, diverse ethnic groups, new and unfamiliar celebrations and festivals and an array of different cultures—it was a new world and a new start indeed!

If all this commotion was just a dream, I needed to wake up. If it was reality, I wanted to understand it, experience it, participate in it, accept its challenges and live it with hope and fulfillment.

As the years moved forward, my focus on living according to our new reality remained unchanged. I endeavoured to achieve my goals with determination, even though I was facing numerous obstacles that intimidated me and invalidated most of my thoughts and objectives with regard to personal achievement.

The content of the following pages is sure to shine some light on the facts and events that shaped my life from early childhood to adulthood and all the way to present day. I know that parts of my journey will sound familiar to many immigrant girls who also made their way from Italy to Canada in the late 1950s or early 1960s. I have written my story to give all the girls who conformed to those stringent house rules and opted to carry their vulnerability throughout their lives a right to be heard.

I cheerfully admit that I made a conscious choice to disentangle myself from those same rigorous rules to go in search of my own greater good. I was determined to brave the unknown and willingly dared to defy those obstacles that were placed before me. I eagerly found a way to pursue my chosen education. I learned about proper business ethics from the best in the field, and eventually I achieved successful entrepreneurship … and I still live the frenzied lifestyle that goes with it.

Today, I feel authenticated. I found an alternative way, and I built a platform that has allowed me to create my own social and economic manifesto. In the end, immigrating to Canada was certainly the right thing for me.

Rose Catalano

A Childs Voyage to New Life

It was the early evening of a brisk and beautiful day in the spring when my parents told me to put my bike away. With frigid palms, my mother helped me change my outfit to something a little more adequate for travel and told me to do my best to keep it tidy. Then, Mom told me to keep an eye on my siblings, Michael and Tony, while she completed a final suitcase count.

Those instructions seemed simple enough, and really, all I had to do was stay put and make sure my little brothers did not go wandering off somewhere or hurt themselves. However, as is often the case with youngsters, rules and instructions are not always followed as directed. When she came to gather the three of us, she started rushing around yelling out the same old question: "Rose, where did you go? Didn't I tell you not to move from here?" I wanted to tell her that we were fine and had not gone very far—we were playing in the next room—but no words came out. As soon as she saw us, I got that familiar look of disapproval, to which I wanted to say: "C'mon mom, what is the problem?" But I remained silent.

Later, I overheard my parents murmuring something about the suitcases being ready. At the same time, they noticed the time on the clock hanging by the wood-burning stove and suggested we best be ready because the cab bound for the seaport in Naples was about to arrive.

As darkness began to fall, I quietly stepped outside and stood on the front steps looking up at the sky. I saw a few shiny stars trying to offer a sign of comfort and reassurance that everything was going to be fine. Feeling reasonably confident with the message from above, I walked back inside. We were all gathered in the large kitchen anxiously awaiting our ride when a lot of family members, neighbours and friends came to bid us farewell and wish us bon voyage. At that split second, I was informed that we were about to go on a journey which would transport us to a faraway place, and it would take about twelve days to reach our destination.

You see, we were a family of five moving with our essentials and bare necessities to start a new life in a land that offered more prosperity and stability (*terra prospera e stabile*). Evidently, all of our baggage made it unnecessarily costly for my parents to arrange the trip by plane, so we were to travel across the ocean by ship and make the rest of the journey by train.

Amid the laughter, the tears and the hugs, I noticed the light beams of a van slowly approaching our home. Suddenly everyone fell silent and mixed emotions triumphed. Within a few short minutes, our bags were loaded, our grandparents gave us more hugs and we drove off into the late night. The drive was long, and the roads were bumpy. We heard the sound of car horns blaring constantly, and the discomfort became more and more intense as I sat with my mother and two siblings in the back seat without an inch of space to allow us any movement. Our bodies almost felt numb, but none of us dared to speak of it.

Finally, after travelling in this cab for what seemed to be almost the whole night, we neared the end of our extended southward drive and arrived safely at the port and in direct view of the gigantic (or so it seemed at the time) ship that would take us to better tomorrows. Could all this really be happening to us?

Crossing the Ocean

There we stood on the dock, stupefied and unfamiliar with our whereabouts. Our luggage was piled next to us, and we stared at the peaceful ocean below for a moment with no feeling of dizziness. My thoughts searched for some direction, but none came. Suddenly, my mind began to flirt with the idea that we could possibly be stranded here for a very long time. In the bewilderment of the moment, my blank stares began jumping from the ocean to the luggage and back again, but nothing seemed to change. No sea creatures emerged from that immense body of water, which to me looked like a stretched-out turquoise horizon egoistically grabbing the reflection of the blue sky above.

Time was standing still; for how much longer, and how were we to make sense of all this?

After what felt like an eternal meaningless wait, this long and silent odyssey was finally interrupted by the arrival of many other groups of adults and children who seemed to be just as misplaced as we were. Together, we patiently waited for the morning sun to stop peeking from a distance and offer itself a jump-start in dismissing its early paleness. Then, without hemming and hawing, I began to do my own arithmetical calculations in an attempt to guess what time that prankster of a Neapolitan sun would press on with the day's brightness.

I did not have any intent to directly question the integrity of my parents' current plans or thoughts, but I covertly wondered if perhaps a directive to them wouldn't have been a noble and most helpful gesture at this stage of the game. However, my thought was only a spontaneous and lonely opinion plucked out of the ocean air, and not of any value to anyone else.

Figuring out what is on people's minds is as difficult as resisting the urge to ask them about their possible contingency plan or if in fact they have a plan in place at all. Armed with this judgment, I got a nonverbal indication that my father must have been on top of things, because not long afterward he left us standing in our segregated spot and in my mother's care while he made his way to the security kiosk. In my father's absence, my mother did her very best to tend to and comfort my two siblings and me, just like she always did.

Shortly thereafter, my father returned, carrying all the validated boarding documentation. Without delay, he expertly began leading us towards the waiting ship. Pretending that everything was making sense, we obediently followed him. As instructed, and without any objections, we quietly made our way to our cabin and, with a slight pause and no option for debate, entered this small, non-air-conditioned, claustrophobic space located on the lower deck.

Skepticism as to the quality of these arrangements surfaced as we walked through different levels and hallways of the ship, encountering along the way a profoundly offensive kitchen odour which instantly insulted our sense of smell and brought on nausea that actually dared to accompany us all the way to Halifax, Nova Scotia. It was so hard to repeat this daily ritual without bursting into tears. Oh, how I loathed that disturbing smell that awaited us each day as we passed along the hallways to reach the dining area.

Unmistakably, the *Vulcania* was not a stylish ship, nor was it a top-of-the-line floating hotel. It was simply the best and most suitable travel means available to my parents. We later found out that this ship was actually retired after our voyage.

In summary, our expedition across the Atlantic Ocean was characteristically unkind. The voyage was harsh, and it made for a frustrating experience. The daily seasickness, dehydration, lack of privacy, worry and sadness led to pronounced and continually unhappy facial expressions that in turn led to our tears leaking like a broken faucet. I was beginning to feel trapped. My eyes fought back tears, my adrenalin was building, and my emotions played at acrobatics while awaiting my decision whether to laugh or cry.

One day, when I thought I had reached my limit, my brain—better known to me as my inner dispatch centre—awakened something in me that began to seek out a way to make all of this stop. Right from the beginning, you could accurately guess that my self-imposed search and rescue mission would not be very rewarding. Eventually, this young girl's mixed emotions were settled by exhaustion that was complemented by sleep. In the end, what I minded most was not being able to find anyone to coach me on how to reassess and improve the gloomy situation we were in. How could I? A child's resources are limited, so I had to alter my objective instead.

As you might guess, this ship did not offer exclusive dining venues, nor did it debut or showcase any superior culinary experiences. Alternative restaurants were not an option. We all dined in one main room equipped with long wooden tables and wooden chairs, and we had no preselected seating arrangements. The ship's décor was unassuming, and to label it elegant or soft on the eye would be incorrect. Within two days, the porthole view from our cabin became my close friend. It offered brief daily distractions as I mulled over the ocean life I had seen that day and anticipated what I might see the next.

The best I can explain those days is that you had to be there to understand how helpless we felt as we shivered at the thought of facing the same smelly congested conditions the next day and for several days after that. We had been caught totally unaware, and the unpleasantness of the situation required sombre tolerance to mask our unhappiness in such a difficult environment. Because I could not remain unaffected throughout this experience, I eventually lost the motivation and the enthusiasm to garner even a small smile so I could show my sparkling white teeth. Although I was far from happy or motivated, however, I was not yet crushed.

With an overwhelming urge not to allow these temporary circumstances a free pass to obscure my mind,

I became totally wrapped up in a fictional place where life was full of enjoyment and happiness. Then, out of the blue and without warning, my subconscious boldly stepped in and nudged me out of my trance. I gave my head a shake and, without wandering any further out of my intensity, I nestled my negative feelings for this affair in a secret spot deep within my memory. There it sat quietly for many long years.

Today, as I look back on this experience, I no longer feel mystified or troubled about it. I can now take a deep breath, and somehow those events from yesterday become utterly inconsequential. I swiftly identify my thoughts that unambiguously confirm my parents had selected a ship that was not fashionable, nor was it trying to win any awards. Without a doubt, the *Vulcania*'s aim was to make good on its assigned duty to take all its passengers to their destination—and that it did.

Frankly, as a result of that emotional journey, I stayed away from cruising for the next forty years. It seems that certain events have a way of remaining trapped in your subliminal mind, and you cannot get rid of them very easily. Eventually, I did succeed in banishing those thoughts, and today cruising has become my vacation of choice. As we know, time is a healer, and therefore life itself must be a phenomenal teacher because, believe it or not,

I eventually grew to understand that even a challenging and bewildering experience like the one I faced as a child could bring about a variety of positive results.

Remarkably, during this demanding journey, my parents met and made friends with other families travelling to the same place for similar reasons and facing the same daunting challenges. This new-found camaraderie aided in the development of strength and harmony, and together we became the benefactors of those qualities for years to come as we celebrated life's occasions and opportunities. Companionship alleviated the daily doldrums and helped the days go by faster.

Canada at Last: Our Arrival in the New Land

Oh my goodness! We had reached day nine of our ten-day ocean journey. Wow! At this point, our situation no longer seemed endless, and our spirits began to lift in anticipation of the announcement that we were reaching land. It was so very important for us to do something awe-inspiring as we were finally landing, so we promptly created a mental postcard illustration of this paradise called Canada that was almost within our reach. In the midst of total excitement for the prospect of landing, we let our hearts fill with eagerness as we paced back and forth, wondering what might be ahead of us.

Then, as the new day dawned and the sun began to shine, the long-awaited tenth day arrived. Our ears promptly and automatically listened for the sound of the loudspeaker message alerting us that we had reached our destination. That sound became my first opportunity to grasp the true meaning of surreal sentiments. Instantly the ship filled with cries of joy and laughter, and something almost hysterical. Amidst all that frenzy, the area seemed to overflow with an immense sense of promise. It was our new beginning.

Everyone started walking with a feeling of urgency towards the gangway, rushing to be the first person to set foot on land. Suddenly, the surge of passengers unexpectedly slowed. As my family and I reached the exit door, I understood why—the ground, as far as our eyes could see, was covered with a white blanket. We squinted in our effort to process this new and unfamiliar vista. My parents and many of the other passengers arriving from a Mediterranean country where snow is seldom present and the temperatures in early April reach the mild level of a thermometer were not quite prepared for the sight of so much snow, nor were we appropriately dressed for the Canadian weather.

That shimmering spectacle became our wake-up call. This unforeseen encounter measured high on our personal Richter scales, inviting bewilderment and disenchantment to temporarily take hold of our senses. My parents looked understandably dismayed; my siblings complained of being hungry and cold, and they pleaded with my parents to take them back home.

Despair seemed to carelessly infringe on our space, gripping adults and children all at the same time. I gave it a few minutes before I asked myself, *how do these people expect a child to understand that a change of surroundings such as this could be the pathway leading to new knowledge, the merriment of new experiences or to part-take in new activities?*

But, it did happen. Fortunately, by the time the next winter came around, we were no longer strangers to accumulations of snow or clouds of it blowing around us. We were overjoyed to watch the large snowflakes drop from the sky and like a ghost land and remain sitting on the edges of the windows. We spent precious minutes watching the snow daringly block the front entrance to the house, and we did not even mind losing the exterior view of the property when huge cascades of white fluff spread right across our visible horizon.

Snow would become for us both a playmate and a nuisance. On the one hand, we were so excited by a snowfall that my siblings, along with my cousins and myself, made opportunities for many "girls against the guys" snowball games. At Christmas time, the packed snow was ideal for contests of who could make a better snowman or who could build the highest snow mountain. Occasionally, the girls got the last word, but we did not fare too well when the snowy conditions came with the responsibility of clearing the driveway. Now snow became a first-rate annoyance.

However, things were quite different the day we landed in Halifax. That day, all I could do was struggle to get my head out of a foreign blur that had me very perplexed. Although I wanted to be of some help to my family, I could not offer any way to make things better for my little brothers. All I could feel was a strange and heavy weight pressing down on me, but I held on with all I had and became totally determined not to let my knees buckle. In an effort not to add to my parents' problems, I just followed along quietly, if begrudgingly.

Through all of these experiences, I was trying to figure out *why*. What had possessed my father to mastermind such a plan, and why had my mother agreed to go along with this preposterous deal? This is what I figured: Adults were the ones in charge, and children were subject to their whims. Within that structure, adults obviously had the power to decide where and how the family lived and who they lived with. Without a doubt, it must have been one of those adults who designed this unreasonable formula. Go figure adults' reasoning or strategies.

Turbulence at the Customs Office

With our backs to the ship and our bodies shivering from the cold weather, we stood before the customs authorities who had diligently and patiently been waiting to greet us. One of them spoke to us in a foreign language, and of course no one understood him. He then switched to the universal language of hand gestures, indicating that we should follow him. This we did.

He led us to a large waiting room and motioned for us to sit down. We all looked at each other, wondering if anyone in the room had any inkling of what the previous message was about. Meanwhile, the customs officers were hoping that their message had successfully been conveyed to at least one or two newcomers. Alas, that was definitely not the case.

Further instructions were spoken, to no one's added enlightenment. Once again, the officers used hand gestures to attempt some form of communication with this crowd whose facial expressions clearly said that whoever invented different languages must not have had serenity in mind. Within a couple of short minutes, I saw a gentleman stand up and begin to follow the agents down a long hallway. They were almost out of sight when my father, along with a few other gentlemen from the group of new arrivals, decided to follow the agents' lead. They auspiciously recognized that this path led them to a ticket counter where they would retrieve the train passes for the prearranged trip to Toronto.

As we sat there waiting for my father to return, we saw several big signs on the walls but had no idea what they said. We quietly continued to sit in attendance for someone to give us yet another hand signal to indicate the next move. By now the situation was becoming not-so-comical in my child's mind, and I wondered why and who had the gall to create different languages that were sure to make some people, mostly us, feel overwhelmed and lost. Wouldn't it be simpler for all the people in the world to practice only one general language, which would act as a universal verbal liberator, instead of dealing with all this foolishness?

Once again, I deduced that adults, being the world's regulators, knew just how to create so many unprecedented inconsistencies that it seriously made you want to blow your top. Just then, a cold shiver came over me, and for some mysterious reason I quickly stifled my irritation as a quiet inner voice told me that the adults in charge were actually clever and legitimate individuals, not phonies without a purpose. Perhaps it was I who did not possess the knowledge to understand it or the insight to see the bigger picture. I had a lot of learning to do.

With nothing else to occupy my time, I lifted my eyes from the floor and, with a blank stare, gazed up at the space around me... and there he was! Finally, my father had returned. He was walking towards us holding two paper bags containing our lunch, and he had a large envelope tucked under his left arm.

He distributed the food and water he had purchased for us and then, with a grin on his face, he showed us the train passes that were enclosed in the white envelope. We were weary, exhausted and reluctant to share in his enthusiasm for more travel, so we did our best to focus on the contents of the paper bags instead. We were hungry, so we hurried to unwrap the lunch and gulp down whatever it contained.

But stop! My brain abruptly requested a few seconds to classify the contents, as it all looked new and different. And then, without putting up a struggle, it gave this food a passing mark. Ironically, when you're especially hungry, not knowing does not translate into not appreciating.

We understood sausage and oven-baked hard-crust bread, but we did not compute hot dogs and soft buns. This was a culture shock. For a short time, though, we felt some contentment thanks to our full stomachs. Perhaps you may wonder what type of person or young child gets all worked up and excited about a hot dog lunch, but for us at that time, we would have eaten almost anything. It didn't much matter what it was.

Negotiating More Travel Adventures

It was soon evident that we would not be riding a magic rail that could call off the upcoming thirty-two-hour train ride to Toronto and snap us there in a few seconds instead. This endless trip kept cutting into our precious play time, and I asked myself if meeting up with my uncle and his family was really going to happen, or was it simply something I didn't understand? I was unable to come up with the correct answer at the time, so I had no choice but continue on our journey with the unanswered question.

In keeping with my parents' streak of reasoning and financial diplomacy, once again our travel accommodation was very basic: sitting-room only. Astonishing! How could they expect three young children to survive this ridiculous ordeal? On the other hand, I was happy to know that we would soon be reunited with our trusted and loved family members, and I figured there was a pretty good chance we would be greeted not only with open arms but with plenty of familiar food waiting for us at their home.

This did not, however, diminish my apprehension about my parents' ability to make sound decisions, because this particular one seemed to be a prime example of what happens when adults arbitrarily decide to uproot all their family members to a foreign land without having the slightest discussion about it with their children. Had they consulted us regarding this gigantic mission, we would definitely have told them to dismiss such folly and stay put, as there was no need for such conclusion.

But, despite the significance of the hardships we encountered while traversing the Atlantic and the intangible feelings of displacement we felt upon landing in a snowy and cold port in Halifax, our energy or lack of, remained focused on completing this escapade with whatever optimism we could master.

One of the things I accurately identified throughout this cavalcade of emotions was the feeling of knowing the person I was and where I came from. Pinpointing where I was going and what the days ahead might be like would have to wait.

All I knew for sure was that I was a little Italian girl removed from her country of birth for reasons I could not put into proper perspective.

In later days, the reality revealed the fact that immigration during the 1950's and 1960's was the outcome of Italy being plagued by vandalism, political unrest, and hate for state controls. On the flip side, I also learned that this little peninsula was well known as an ancient place full of historic artifacts and deeply rich in architecture, splendid beaches, excellent food and superb fashion. In short, Italy had class, good cheese, excellent wines and lots of stylish clothes. This jewel was home to super stars like Versace, Gucci, Armani, Feragamo, Pucci and many others.

Yes, this was the country I left behind, and yes, I would never forget it.

As solemnly promised to myself, I eventually returned to Italy to savor the beauty of its iconic structures such as the Coliseum, The Vatican, The Forum, the striking scenery of Venice, the Basilica of St. Francis in Assisi, the Renaissance riches of Florence and the Leaning Tower of Pisa. Of great importance to me was the significant exquisiteness of the sites I visited in the southern regions of Puglia and Calabria. Of course, southern Italy is where my home was. Below, I share some of the most interesting places I had the pleasure to visit.

Enjoying a drink of fresh water in the mountainous plateau of "**La Sila"** located in the region of Calabria. The first known settlers of this plateau were the Bruttii. Later it was occupied by the Byzantines and by the 16th century, Albanians had settled this area in the direction of the Ionian Sea. In the late 19th century, La Sila was annexed to Italy. For the longest time, this isolated forested plateau served as a safe haven for wolves and gangs of robbers.

Today, La Sila has become a tourist attraction in the summer and a skiing resort in the winter.

"Trulli" are dry stone houses located in Alberobello, a region of Puglia. During the 17th century a Trullo was a home for peasant families who could not afford to pay the heavily imposed taxes from the nobility of the time. The dwellings afforded the peasant owners the upper hand to demolish the home without much notice simply by pulling the roof-stone out. People could make the house disappear faster than the tax man could show up with an extended hand demanding to collect the dues.

These circular houses typically measure approximately 9' wide by 6' high and are built from limestone rocks. Their thick walls help to keep the Trullo cool in the summer and warm in the winter. Most of the Trulli have only one room under the pointed roof. Children sleep in alcoves made in the wall. Privacy is achieved by hanging a curtain in front of the bed.

Since the late 1990's, the Trulli have welcomed many tourists - in particular visitors from Britain and Germany.

“Segezia,” a rural township founded in 1938 during the Fascist reform era. The name comes from the Latin *Seges,* which means agricultural or planted fields. Back in the day and under Mussolini’s control, Segezia was intended to become a new fascist city, however, the project was abandoned with the rise of the Republic.

The Church of Our Lady of Fatima with the depiction of the Madonna and Child on the front portal remains a main attraction. Also to be appreciated is the nine floor square bell tower that stands alone in the large churchyard.

Currently, the occupational resources of the village are kept revitalized by its residents as they adjust to new social and economic realism.

"Orsara di Puglia," a southern town of about 2,800 inhabitants and home to my maternal grandparents. My mother and my father were both raised here.

This picturesque little town sits about 600m above sea level and is surrounded by a river to the east, a stream to the north and mountains to the south and the west. It is unknown if the name "Orsara" was derived from the large presence of bears *(orso)* or from *Ursus,* a Byzantine personality.

During the 8th century, a group of Basilian monks settled here and worshipped the Archangel Michael in a cave which today has become a pilgrimage. Another prominent monument of this town is the fountain of the Angel "Fontana dell'Angelo" which supplies drinking water to the people. Orsara is also renowned for its excellent cuisine and each year it hosts many patrons from surrounding cities. The streets and buildings are well maintained to keep an inviting impulse on food and wine tourism.

"Polignano a Mare," a town settled since prehistoric times. It is located in the southern part of Italy (near the city of Bari) on the Adriatic Sea. Some believe this is the site of Neapolis, an ancient Greek city.

The well being of the local economy is dependent mostly on tourism, fishing and some agriculture.

“Capo Colonna” is the last standing column of the Temple of Hera Lacinia located near Crotone, in the region of Calabria. This Archaeological park is made up of approximately 30 hectares of land used for excavation purposes. It is believed this sacred sanctuary was dedicated to Hera the wife and sister of Zeus, the protector of women, fertility and family. Artifacts found in this park are displayed in the museum located at the front entrance.

"Santa Severina" a steeple city placed on a high rocky cliff and protected by defensive walls. A castle looks down at a town of approximately 2,000 inhabitants in Crotone. It is speculated that at one time the castle was under the rule of the Bourbons.

Several excavations conducted in and around 2008 have brought to light the discovery of caves and cemeteries along with a Byzantine church buried below the castle.

Exterior laundry area still standing in a small village of Cosenza in Calabria. Women from the nearby villages would gather here to hand-wash their clothes in free running cold water.

Acknowledging What Was

Back in Italy, we had lived in a facility comprised of multiple acres of agricultural land and a two-story building complex shared by a number of family members. Our paternal grandparents had their own apartment located approximately 200 metres (220 yards) from the main building, and my maternal grandparents lived in a small town a short distance away. Our property was located approximately 10 kilometres (just over 6 miles) from the main city of Foggia and about 2.5 kilometres (1.5 miles) from the small town of Segezia in a southern region of Italy. Life was simple, and the families knew how to live within their means. We enjoyed the fresh air and always made full use of the outdoors.

In those days, we did not worry much about global warming or the possible dangers of continued exposure to high UV rays. The property was enriched with grapevines, fruit orchards, vegetable patches, grains and olive trees. Livestock was plentiful and well cared for, and the oversized exterior grounds and the barn were used as a shared facility. Each family respected the other's space—although, as stories go, sometimes the sharing was not managed very well and resulted in questionable adult behaviour.

As my mother tells it, in the event that such incidents happened and the disagreements failed to come to a hasty resolution, my grandfather became the self-appointed bargaining agent and saw to it that his self-proclaimed expertise in conflict resolution was applied according to his own unique standards. He would, without hesitation, take matters into his own hands by showing up with a rifle, ready to settle the score his way. He offered a convincing alternative that always got results. It was a little unconventional, to say the least, but it worked.

To my grandfather, long conversations were redundant. He was creative in his way of helping others make the most of every minute of the day rather than waste precious time on useless worries. I would describe my grandfather as introverted, very analytical and capable of making gut-driven decisions. He was a veteran who had served with the infantry during World War I. He did not speak metaphorically, and he held serenity and honesty as sacred virtues. Of vast importance to him was his desire to leave behind a chronicle of his life experiences in the hope of teaching his grandchildren to be mindful of each other, especially during hard times.

His talking points came particularly alive in the winter months, when he proudly gathered all the grandchildren, sat us around his wood-burning stove and—once he was comfortable that we were ready for story time—proceeded to tell us about his war experiences, which were marked by melancholic hardships. With great precision, he detailed the fears that threatened to engulf his regiment and the gallantry required to overcome the chaotic suffering and some very painful memories. He always spoke with a frosty voice and heartfelt expression about the total conviction and unending physical and mental endurance that made it possible for him to survive and recover from his two enemy-inflicted injuries. He was always so proud to show us his scars.

I still recall how he pointed out to us the courage he and his comrades exhibited when, equipped only with bayonets, they fiercely fought the enemy in close proximity in one last determined effort to save Northern Italy from enemy occupation. Their mission was to save it at all costs. And they did it with passion in their hearts.

Unfortunately, most of us were too young at the time to comprehend the meaning of his history lessons, and we were definitely not mature enough to respect the worth of the detailed information he was trying to pass on to us. Consequently, at times we came across as disinterested and uninvolved brats who poked fun at his lectures and laughed at the incidents that were closest to his heart.

Evidently, the passion in his words was not absorbed, interpreted or digested appropriately by such young kids. If I had an opportunity to change the past, I would most definitely listen intently and give my grandfather thumbs up for being my hero. I distinctly remember one of his narratives that has remained with me through all these years. It is the incident of one of his eagle-eyed comrades who, while on patrol duty one winter evening, quietly spotted a foreign sentry lighting a cigarette. He wrongly assumed that the enemy was alone, and his patriotic optimism steered him towards a surprise attack.

My grandfather's comrade felt quite confident that overpowering the sentry would be just like another exercise in combat training. He figured with this manoeuvre and a true act of heroism, he would exponentially weaken the enemy's position, and in return he would definitely receive a medal and a short leave away from that treacherous battleground.

Unfortunately, things did not go as he had planned, and the soldier suffered a series of bone fractures and severe head injuries. That unanticipated outcome definitely took him away from the battleground, but not on his terms. It was a long time before our grandfather's comrade could be nursed back to reasonable health, even though the nurses and doctors worked tirelessly to keep him alive and in some form of controlled pain. In those days, the infirmary barracks were not always adequately stocked with drugs, medical equipment or disinfecting supplies.

For my grandfather, this incident was not something to be made fun of. Gauging our disconnect and disregard for the significance of this episode, he ordered us to leave his house at once, and he made sure our departure was effected with the speed of light. I remember one other time when I ran out so fast that I left my shoes behind. My mother went to collect them for me the next day.

Another moving memory was of my grandfather telling us about a young man who had grown very attached to him during their mountain warfare in the Alps and the Dolomites. The harsh winter conditions and uneven terrain made their mission extremely difficult as they dug trenches for protection against the Hungarian and Austrian army and to gain some slight semblance of respite. The two of them supported each other and took to sharing clothing and food to keep their spirits alive, because the manner of combat in such high altitudes was so drastic that quite often it broke the soldiers' morale.

Imagine the bruised feelings these combatants experienced as they watched the cable cars bring food and armaments up to the soldiers who were stationed on the mountaintops and then, from the corner of their eye, steal a glimpse as the same cars make their way back down carrying their wounded or departed friends. One miserable day, after two months of facing this unrelenting enemy, shells were detonating in every direction when an avalanche came down, separating several soldiers from their battalion. When my grandfather realized his friend was nowhere in sight, he went to search for him, and he found him just as he was taking his last breath. That traumatic moment left our *nonno* emotionally injured and extremely angry.

What had fate done to them?

Wouldn't you know, my father was present when this story was being told, and when my grandfather mentioned how he and the departed soldier shared their limited supplies, my father's impertinence kicked in and he boldly asked my grandfather what percentage of the goods had been allocated to him. With that remark, my grandfather sparked like a firecracker and, in his anger, picked up the closest object and threw it at my father. He hit the target dead centre. That heavy, outsized loaf of stone-baked bread delivered a stern and clear message: Nobody is permitted to have fun at a fallen soldier's expense. No one at all, and for no reason at all.

My father never admitted it, but I believe he learned an important lesson that day. We certainly took note of it too. None of us was laughing after such a critical episode.

The Power of Reminiscence

While we were still sifting through the everlasting confusion at the train station in Halifax in preparation for boarding the train for Toronto, my siblings and I felt lost and helpless. Our efforts to decipher why we were even here in this strange country made us feel like we were staring down an abyss. We could see no end in sight.

One of my brothers had by now reached the peak of his agitation level, and he loudly vocalized his discontent. I too felt a shadow looming above me in a form bigger than anything I had ever dealt with before. However, I chose a different avenue for myself and let my mind dash back to our home, the place I knew so well. I envisioned the people

I was missing. Wishful thinking and daydreaming can sometimes be a child's best friend.

This time my thoughts brought me back to my paternal grandmother, who was a woman of strength and character. She was always there to cheer us on no matter what we were trying to accomplish. She understood my grandfather well, recognized that he did not accept any form of criticism, always made light of situations she knew would not be received kindly by him and came up with a solution before he was made aware of the problem. She was his source of strength and a positive enabler who made their lives run without too many hiccups.

He silently acknowledged that she was a competent and very advanced woman, even though such words were never spoken. What a team! She liked to party, told jokes, enjoyed singing, worked hard, was a strict disciplinarian and believed in the value of education. My grandmother was described by all those who knew her as an emancipated woman who, in the late 1940s, truly enjoyed her time away for mud baths and expertly crafted her own version of the suffragette movement. She was a woman of moral fibre and valour.

She was actively involved with the family business, and I am told that after she gave birth to each of her fourteen children—all delivered at home without much or any medical assistance—she resumed work as usual after two short days of rest. Regrettably, in that era, meningitis had no scruples, and seven of her children were taken away in infancy.

After some years, for her, distance was almost as much a culprit as death when it came to the loss of her children. Perhaps a kin's loss to distance does not impact as much as death does, but it is a loss nonetheless. The day her youngest son turned 16, he made an announcement that changed the family dynamics. My grandmother was left standing in the middle of the room lock-handed and in disbelief. She double-checked the message that her son had delivered in three short seconds, and to prevent any mayhem, she held back any interrogation. Her son was leaving the family to make a new start as an apprentice mechanic in Venezuela. This was another emotional blow to add to her already heavily distressed baggage. She probably did not get a lot of sleep that night, but never once did she put her own feelings ahead of his desire.

A few years later, another son uprooted his young family and moved to Canada, and three years after that, we followed in their footsteps and joined them in Toronto. She knew it would be a very long time before she saw any of us again, if time even allowed such a reunion. Still, her very strong character did not permit her to surrender to her enormous pain, nor did it grant room for a quest to unearth justification for these unkind losses. She always soldiered on full steam ahead, internalizing her pain and storing it to be dealt with in silence and on her own terms.

Fortunately, although nonna's family was now divided, family members never lost contact—with her or each other. Emigrating to a foreign country did not denote they would never meet again. Not only did the postal service get a good workout delivering written communication to and from my grandparents' headquarters, but all three sons made more than one trip back to visit with their parents until such time as nature designated their final goodbyes.

From the beginning of my grandparents life together, it was well understood and agreed that their accumulation of heartbreaking emotional hurdles would not authorize or mete out any extra softness to their surviving six boys and one girl to compensate for the tragic loss of their infant children.

All their children were taught family values, courage and the willingness to survive and succeed. As years went by and the children grew up to be young men and a young lady, my grandmother busied herself to make sure they appreciated competitiveness. They participated in and assisted my grandfather with the agricultural business, shared the responsibility for the care of the livestock and, most of all, knew how to have a good time. She believed that you do not take a back seat and then be left wondering what the heck just happened. Effectiveness and competence were not just words to her; they had to be transformed from talk to action. She did that effectively.

For the most part, things had been progressing well for my grandparents, and business was profitable. Unfortunately, once World War II broke out, life as they knew it took a dramatic turn. They faced the distinct possibility that their sons would be called to arms and they would be forced to re-live the nightmares and face similar hardships they had suffered and endured during the First World War.

Spared by the fact that they owned and managed a large agricultural property, one of the sons was exempted from service, as he was deemed necessary house labour, and therefore he had to remain engaged in the operation of the business. Two of the six sons and the daughter were very young, so they remained at home, whereas three of the older sons were drafted. One of the sons called to the service was my father. He was assigned to the infantry, and his two brothers were in aviation. Fortunately, after months and years of agony and despair, armistice saw that all three boys returned home alive, but they were not unscathed.

During her sons' time away in the service, my grandmother did her utmost to get through the barriers of enemy soldiers in an effort to send them parcels containing chocolates, cigarettes, socks and anything else she could gather. Those were dark times for the family and for the farming industry. As is typical during wartime, the Italians were not sheltered from staggering blows delivered by enemy soldiers who were instructed not to be considerate of people or property. Destruction was lurking everywhere, food was scarce and fears of personal attacks were plenty.

Young females were especially in danger of rape or physical abuse. Most people would hide their daughters and sometime their wives in the attic in an effort to avoid aggression. Sometimes it worked, and other times the men were beaten until they disclosed the hiding spots. I graphically remember my grandfather talking about the perilous encounters he experienced as he witnessed convents being raided, food being confiscated and nuns suffering personal abuse.

Civilians were no match for such ruthless military operations. The government dispensed its authority to curb hostilities through the use of ex-military personnel known as the Black Shirts, whose motto was "I don't give a damn" (*non me ne frega niente*), but it could still do nothing to prevent those atrocities.

From the onset of the war, my grandmother did her best to learn a miniscule bit of English so she could slightly converse with the advancing solders in the hope of averting or at least minimizing the damage inflicted on her household as they ravaged her home taking whatever food was in sight. The enemy frequently left nonna and her family members in short supply. Her version of the communication went something like this: "Whatta you wonn? You wonn tis?" After their demands were met, the soldiers nodded, said goodbye and walked away. She showed them no fear and acknowledged their leaving with a quick "Byee byee." Once the soldiers exited the gate of the premises, my grandmother would complete her response in private by adding, "You sanimabeech!" And then she would walk away with her head held high, singing her self-scripted songs.

Another major concern that aroused fear in my grandmother's heart was the attitude of her not-so-conciliatory and most argumentative second eldest son. He was known to be profoundly disobedient. He had a passion for defiance against authority, detested that unfathomable war and was of a most uncooperative nature. To him, she constantly wrote letters emphasizing the benefits of collaboration with his superiors. She asked him to refrain from questioning their leadership style.

But, not to her surprise, she was often informed that he was being disciplined or in the lock-up as a result of his insubordination. The reality of it was that during those most unnerving and dangerous times, my uncle's revolutionary nature ultimately kept him away from having to handle a firearm or face enemy lines. Perhaps that was not such a bad trade-off!

A Lesson in Times Gone By

As history had previously taught the Italian population, war is seldom designed to be reasonable or kind, and this one came with the added anxiety of communism. Italians clearly understood that being antimilitary did not serve to aid or protect their opportunities for growth. It only brought them to a fork in the road, pondering which path to take as they attempted to denounce occupation, Fascism and Socialism. These struggles and a multitude of other war hardships came in many different shapes and forms, consequently raising doubt in the minds of the public about the eventual outcome.

Finally, after a long and menacing period of turmoil and a never-ending struggle to survive, the war ended and our family was harmoniously reunited. However, not all families were so lucky. Many good people were left with only memories of their husbands, sons, brothers, fathers and, in some shocking cases, daughters. This was a time that offered no reassurance, nor were people ready or strong enough to engage in any real conversations about their harsh conditions or their struggle to keep putting one foot in front of the other as they wept over their tragic losses.

It seemed that they were only capable of verbally and emotionally conveying a mixture of broken emotions and incorrect facts. People struggled to come to grips with all they had witnessed, and in light of what they were continuing to bear, they could only envision a deck that did not stack up in their favour. Their farms and homes had been decimated without mercy, their family units were torn apart, social unrest loomed everywhere and the will to carry on appeared to be a vain exercise without any meaningful end result.

But the sun came up the next day, and life went on. My grandfather being a man with a vivid business mind dared to perceive this critical situation as an opportunity for growth. With full empathy for the pain and losses suffered by a great number of people—and with no disrespect for the more disadvantaged folks—he saw fit to release the handbrakes that had long stalled his business development plan. With modest simplicity, he drafted a clever and detailed incremental agricultural action plan that would once again promote concrete results. His was a theme that symbolized renewed hope for economic success, and it came with a long list of "must do," "must not do," "go for it" and "need more time to assess." Obviously, he did not believe in snappy or dramatic operational plans.

Together, the family worked hard and with vital enthusiasm to achieve the end goal as set out by the leader of the pack. To my grandfather's credit, the mission was a success. Even in the face of all dogmatic political dilemmas, compounded by economic and personal disruptions, my grandfather's plan proved to be sustainable and managed to gain momentum. With the help of the generous fertility of the soil, the abundance of harvested crops cleared the way for robust sales, and after a few years of continued hard work and identifiable success, my grandfather made another calculated and sensible expansion. This time, he purchased additional agricultural property located much closer to the main city of Foggia.

This acquisition offered ease of grain transportation and superior market exposure for the sales of milk, eggs and other produce. He assigned the management of this location to his eldest son, Michael. In my eyes, my grandfather will remain a man with vision and a management technique that showed he knew how to turn time into money.

At the same time, the nation was ripe for more economic growth and expansion in product manufacturing. Of course, this translated into large demands for new roads, railroads, highways, dams and power plants.

Since most of the industrial development was taking place in northern Italy, the south experienced serious migration to cities like Milan, Turin and Genoa. Another factor that contributed to the mass migration was that the labourers from the south came at a more affordable cost. One would think that this movement would be the key to creating conditions to benefit the working class, but instead it promoted complete disregard for people and property. Repression and parasitism were rampant as Italy dipped into political disorder. The year 1945 was, among other things, a time that saw obstinate gypsies refuse to integrate into society. They chose to freely roam the country in unmarked caravans, stealing farming equipment, bicycles, food, clothing, logs, blankets and whatever else they could get their hands on. Then they disappeared without a trace.

They had such flawed standards that it was common for them to relieve themselves out in the open and in full view of men, women and children and think nothing of it. They also excelled in property thrashing and pick-pocketing.

Gypsies effectively capitalized on current public discontent without fear of incarceration or punishment, as the authoritarian law enforcer/dictator Benito Mussolini had faced total defeat and had subsequently met his demise.

Might it be this society who taught us the phrase, "you've been gypped?"

Adopting One's Own Safety Measures

As a young adult without a thought of avoidance of work, my father willingly and energetically helped with the administration of my grandfather's growing estate while also allowing himself time to pursue his preferred social activities. One of his prime social goals was to meet a suitable girl he could eventually make his wife.

Before long, he met my mother, who was immediately smitten by his looks—although she quickly recognized he had the capacity to be snappy, had a tendency to be a risk taker and exercised the kind of frankness with the use of the language commonly attributed to a street fighter. Still, those personal characteristics were not enough to change her mind.

Naturally, when my mother discussed with her parents her encounter with my father and her feelings for him, she was quickly made aware that they were familiar with his large family unit, his father's progressive business endeavours and the family's reputation for being somewhat impulsive. Needless to say, they were not so much moved by the news as they were concerned about their young daughter's ability to adapt to such a new-fangled environment. Clearly, they believed they knew better, and they made several attempts to introduce her to other suitors who, in their opinion, were a healthier match for her.

My mother, who by nature was—and still is—a person not known to be any kind of a rebel, took a stand this one time, and six months later she and my father were married. Her parents attended the ceremony with a heavy heart and were tentative with their blessings. A year later I was born, and there was finally a truce between my maternal grandparents and my parents.

My mother had by now been away from the safety of her parents' nest for a while and was doing her best to adjust and adapt to the faster pace of her new environment. She was learning to be a mother while at the same time caring for the house and the livestock, and participating in field duties when my father became overwhelmed. In her words, she now understood the practical elements her parents had been concerned about. But despite some obvious challenges, she continued to move forward, never settling for half quantity or short measures. If and when my mother did experience any painful crisis, my paternal grandmother was always quick to lend a hand and dish out encouragement as well as expert advice.

Almost on the day I turned two, my first brother was born, and seven years after that another brother came along. Now with a family of five and a lot of work to be done, my parents designated me as the free live-in sitter for my younger brothers. Of course, my babysitting duties came without reward. It was simply expected of me to ensure the safety and well-being of my two siblings, no questions asked. For the most part, even though sometimes this responsibility infringed on my personal playtime, I will concede that I benefitted from the experience, and I was pleased to rise to the occasion.. On the whole, my parents found their hard work quite fulfilling and to some extent even rewarding.

For them, however, the prolonged period of national and social unrest, marked by the news of frequent and unprovoked hostilities against people and property, seemed to offer bleak hope for law and order to soon be restored to the land. Such absence of national and political discipline was the cause of sudden morale shifts for many honest citizens. This external, unwarranted and uncontrolled behaviour gave rise to feverish nightmares for business owners who endeavoured to nurture and protect their property from vandalism. It was obvious and not surprising that the typical landowner did not deal very well with such dysfunctional circumstances.

It would be a long time before some form of governmental control would be established and prove itself competent enough to draw up new and seriously needed laws. In the meantime, faced with constant daily intimidation, many owners of agricultural property developed security measures of their own, arming themselves with pistols and rifles in an effort to safeguard against theft of their livestock and grain. All the while, the brazen thieves were unashamedly awarding themselves *carte blanche*. My father was among the vigilantes who habitually patrolled their property at night with definite resolve. Nevertheless, all his brash determination did not bamboozle him into thinking that his presence alone was enough to deter criminal activity on his premises.

Because peasant poverty did not diminish as hoped, it became evident that my family's property would soon become a marked target. My father, along with his two guard dogs, maintained constant and resolute watch over his property for a long time. However, his vigilance only delayed and annoyed the would-be perpetrators who had arrogantly eyed this commission. It wasn't long before they upped their game in an effort to accomplish their undertaking.

In the early hours of one moonlit spring morning, the guard dogs dutifully alerted my father that all was not well. Immediate wide-awake action from my father was warranted, and without hesitation, he jumped out of bed, threw on some clothes and with gun in hand cautiously inched his way towards the barn. Suddenly he came in full view of an armed man pointing a weapon right at him as two others ran away.

This really was an unfavourable position for my father to be in. He quickly realized that he had no time to assess the predicament he was in, nor did it seem to be in his best interest to attempt to do so. Survival instincts kicked in, and he reacted with the only possible choice that was available to him. He aimed his gun and fired.

The gun jammed, and, fortunately the other party had a rapid change of heart. Instead of firing at my father, he lowered his weapon and made a run for it. Perhaps the perpetrator thought he might be up against a crazy individual who was even more of a risk taker than he was, so he elected to abandon his foiled plan and return another night with a more plausible one.

It seems that the latter was precisely what the thief had in mind. Two months after this incident occurred, despite all their prodigious vigilance, my parents woke up one rainy morning to find all their livestock gone, including the chickens. This time, the perpetrators not only completed their task with success; they were shameless enough to leave behind one chick with a scribbled note attached to its neck that said: "You are too young. We will be back for you later."

This most inopportune and ruthless incident hit my father so hard that he not only felt a personal defeat but saw this as a loss of freedom and he also lost his spirit. In his mind, the gravity of such insensitivity completely robbed decent hard-working citizens of their right to exercise their potential without the incessant threat of heartbreak. Inevitably, this became my parents' solemn distress, and before long it led to many intense conversations about the possibility of emigrating to new and more stable lands.

Conforming to this inadequate form of national safety and security was negatively affecting our family values, and it did not seem to be a strategically sound option any longer. In essence, they concluded that it was time to seek out industrialized countries that encouraged compliance with laws and had reasonable governmental controls in place.

Since my father's younger brother and his family had left Italy a few years earlier to embark on a fresh start in Canada, my parents decided to consult with them. Without delay, the two parties initiated interesting and confidential communication thoroughly outlining the legal requirements for emigrating to Canada, probable employment prospects, budgeting methods and practical accommodation for a family of five. They also discussed education, medical care, weather conditions and the cost of living as compared to Italy. Together, they developed the most efficient plan for a successful migration. The crucial question here is, how did they really know they were right? I can only conclude that their plan was reinforced by discipline, passion, courage and the fact that there was already some family there to support us.

And so, the necessary budget was established, along with the plan to uproot the family and move to Canada. It was a meaningful life change. Figuring that personal betterment was not guided by destiny or luck alone, my parents took charge of the situation and gave my uncle the green light to proceed with the sponsorship arrangements, knowing full well that this was a process that would easily take one to two years to come to fruition.

The wheels were put in motion, and of course the arrangements had to be kept totally secret until, after approximately a year, the visas were issued and received. Prudence and experience dictated that it was wise to keep such plans locked in a dark and hidden spot. At the time, the political situation was in such upheaval that anyone could easily destroy your plans by reporting you as an active member of the troubled Communist Party. The probability of these people wasting their time and closing your doors to emigration was of great alarm. The other problem was that if such a report was made, no questions would be asked, and no actual verification was required. Your fate would be sealed, and you would not leave.

Given this circumstance, confidentiality was crucial. It must have been a difficult task for my parents to keep silent until the day all the pieces came together. The end result must have brought them some joy knowing that they had played a good hand in that particular poker game.

Reaching Our Final Destination

Oh! Wait a minute, Mom said we only have five hours left on the train. Four hours. Three hours. Two … and here we are! We heard the brakes squeal, and then the train slowed down till it came to a full stop. *Really? We have actually arrived in Toronto? What an endless ride that was, and now it is dark again.*

We stepped onto the station platform and scanned the brightly lit area for familiar faces. It was almost impossible to make any clear distinctions as a multitude of people buzzed around like drunken bees. We stood there for a few more minutes scouring the area and hoping that this big mass of people would be good enough to disappear fairly soon. Suddenly, we were spotted by three of our family members, who wasted no time rushing towards us. With smiles that stretched ear to ear, they affectionately and officially welcomed us to Toronto.

Without a moment's delay, the adults collected our luggage, and we made our way to the parked vehicle that was our mode of transportation to our new home. It was a monstrous beige vehicle that to me looked more like a small airplane named "Pontiac" than a car. The engine started as soon as the key ordered it to, and within a few brief minutes, we accelerated from the parking spot to the expressway that was still a few miles away from our destination—our family's new home.

As the car effortlessly travelled the well-paved road, I could not believe how smoothly this big vehicle moved through the accommodating streets. You see, where we came from, the main roads were somewhat challenging and not very wide. They were comprised of two fairly narrow lanes (one each way), and the most common means of transportation were bus, bicycle or motorcycle. Only the most affluent few drove an Alfa Romeo, and the well-to-do drove a Fiat 500, which measured about the size of the trunk of this monstrous vehicle.

Motoring at a respectable speed, we drove past numerous high-rise buildings on one side of the highway and a variety of commercial buildings on the other, as symmetrically positioned street lights provided visual aid to the drivers throughout their nocturnal journey. Traffic seemed to move along smoothly and effortlessly on that multi-lane stretch of road. All this was accomplished without the constant sound of the horns blaring every other second for no apparent reason. My young mind supposed Canadians must be very sensitive to noise pollution.

What also caught my immediate attention was the diligence exercised by the drivers as I watched the more obedient stop at red lights. I was astonished to notice that pedestrians totally obeyed the road signs. I did not see anyone scurrying out of the way to avoid having his or her feet clipped off by speeding vehicles while crossing the road on a green light. *Wow*, I thought, *this is not the way we get around in Italy! I think I'm going to like this orderly structure.* Just then, a vehicle marked "police" passed us. *What were these two men selling?* I wondered. In Italy, a *police* is a flea. Later, it was explained to me that the police are the *polizia.*

Uh! I think this new world is going to necessitate a lot of learning on our part. I wonder if, in their decision-making swiftness, my parents even stopped to consider the probability that adapting to the new and the different could be a rather stressful and nerve-racking experience for adults and children alike. Or, had someone fooled them into believing that the process was relatively easy and quite effortless to achieve?

Already, any attempt at ineffective communication seemed to suggest we would definitely be facing a number of cumbersome situations in the days to come. In fact, for the next several months, our lack of language comprehension left us totally stupefied and pushed us squarely outside our comfort area. There were times when the thought of opportunity for growth and prosperity simply was not enough to take our eyes off that lingual focal point. I still remember the feelings of frustration I endured and my failed struggles to advance brought on from the inability to converse in English. Hand gestures would sometime provide some slight consolation, but, it did not erase the feeling of inadequacy. Furthermore, when that speechless communiqué method failed, we often became the subjects of laughter and ridicule because we had not successfully made the dialogue grade.

Our New Domicile

At last we were home. When the car pulled into the driveway of a three-bedroom bungalow, I noticed that this property was substantially smaller than what I was accustomed to, and for sure it was unable to accommodate a stable with horses. How could it? The front lawn measured a fraction of the playground we had enjoyed back home, and the neighbours' homes on either side were sitting way too close to my uncle's property.

I was taking it all in and forming my opinion, and here's what my young girl's mind made of it: I immediately resented the location and size of the windows, which seemed to pose a threat to my privacy and extend an open invitation for peeping Toms to have a field day at my expense. Who and what type of builder could have been so malicious as to sell his soul for this type of unwarranted corruption? Had anyone wisely done statistical calculations or research on this problematic set-up?

Then I remembered that we had left a property that was situated approximately 300 metres (328 yards) from the next home, with a dividing space filled with fruit trees and grapevines. In my eyes, this new panorama appeared to be a lot less spacious and slightly claustrophobic. Who said size doesn't matter? At this point, I just didn't get the meaning of this much smaller separation.

We were hastily escorted inside the house and I immediately saw a rectangular table my aunt had kindly preset for dinner. Oh! How we cheered at that long-anticipated sight. The aroma of familiar food now overshadowed all previous events. This moment marked the end of our never-ending journey. We ate plenty and with fervour. We also dared to drink something we had never seen or heard of before: ginger ale. It was not like the Italian *gazzosa* or *chinotto*, but we sure liked it.

When dinner was done, we—the yawning children—were shown to the bedroom while the adults engaged in conversation. The next morning, we got up a little more refreshed, slightly energetic and definitely not as restless. My aunt had prepared breakfast for us, and we indulged very happily. We were helping ourselves to that well-prepared buffet when we noticed that the spread contained another item that was foreign to us; doughnuts! This is what I afterwards called our gluttony encounter with food that knew no boundaries.

As the days wore on, our sense of taste became familiar with the flavour of Lipton chicken soup, popcorn, potato chips and Jell-O. These were some of the foreign delights we were discovering, savouring and relishing. Life was getting better!

Changes and Complexities

Now it was time for the adults to methodically discuss the best way to move forward, and they unanimously agreed that it would be beneficial for all of us to spend a few days at home for a little orientation with the local infrastructure, including medical services, public transportation, shopping areas, enrolment for school-aged children, babysitting for the youngest and employment for my parents. This was necessary information that, when properly put in place, would provide practical guidelines for us, the new immigrants.

We all understood and appreciated that in moving forward, this knowledge would smooth the progress of embracing and engaging in this local community life. It was a new life that had new meaning for all of us. With our fresh points of reference, we did not feel scared or nervous to see a Jamaican family living across the street or a lady with a headscarf (*hijab*) walking towards the bank.

There was an enormous accumulation of new facts, new experiences and unfamiliar activities that we thought of as the "positive anxiety" (*forza positiva*) of living in this new world. We also learned that my uncle and aunt had been proactive—my uncle had managed to procure a job in construction for my father, and my aunt had arranged for my mother to work with her in a factory.

When Monday morning came, my parents headed out to work as planned. My brother and I proceeded to go to grade school, accompanied by our cousin Mary; my youngest sibling went to the preselected babysitter. At the end of the day, we gathered for dinner. Sad to say, the main topic of our conversation was, "I feel so lost. I did not understand anything anyone said to me, and now we have to do this all over again tomorrow?"

After two weeks of feeling useless and frustrated, my father returned home rather late one evening and was visibly distraught about an event that had made work an unpleasant and difficult ordeal for him that morning. We sympathized with him when we noticed his struggle to contain his built-up anger as he prepared to tell us about the incident that had made his day a true nightmare. We listened carefully and with complete interest as he proceeded to explain how in the first hour of the morning his foreman tried to train him on how to use the fire extinguisher in the event it was ever needed. In his eagerness to show his boss that he understood the gist of the procedures (pull, aim, squeeze and sweep), he actually pulled the pin and squeezed the top lever.

Of course, in doing so, he unintentionally discharged the extinguisher, and to add insult to injury, since there was no fire to aim it at, he threw the extinguisher on the floor. Not knowing what else he could do, he stood there, frozen, watching the foam make a mess of the place. He literally felt his emotions slipping into a catatonic state.

His co-workers burst into hysterical laughter as they waited for the safety device to empty so they could assist with the cleanup. They actually did not mind the idea of a couple of hours off work. Erroneously, my father misread their intended gestures. Figuring they were laughing at him rather than sympathizing with him, he ran outside, collected a bunch of stones and hurled them at the co-workers. Faced with my father's faultless aim, his well-intentioned co-workers had to duck for cover.

Luckily, the labour laws of the time were not as defined as they are today, so he did not receive any disciplinary action. His boss felt that he had suffered enough punishment through the humiliation of the incident and gave him the benefit of the doubt, believing that this was an isolated incident brought on by embarrassment rather than intentional disregard for safety in the workplace.

His boss also recognized that my father had potential and, with that gut feeling, he did one more helpful thing; he recommended that my father be transferred to the roofing unit, where he could work for a foreman who spoke a little Italian. The following week, his transfer was approved, and the reassignment was achieved. It was there that he flourished, and he continued to be an asset to the company for a good many years. He happily welcomed that change and complemented it by investing in a book of English/Italian translations, with which he taught himself enough broken English to enable him to communicate adequately.

My mother also experienced issues in the workplace due to her lack of knowledge of the English language, but her dilemma had more to do with the unintended slower production as a result of her not comprehending the instructions. Management was not pleased with this situation, so they had someone physically show her what and how the product was to be assembled, how to stack the skids and also how to seal and label the boxes for shipping. For numerous days, she endured irritation and frustration brought on by negative thoughts because she was unable to explain her lingo disadvantage to her immediate supervisor. Her boss showed no empathy for her situation and had little or no tolerance for any delays in production. My mother coped with those difficulties for a few months and then moved on to work for another factory, where she joined a few other Italian-speaking employees. This proved to be a much less stressful environment, and the atmosphere was certainly more conducive to successful productivity. Even though her earnings were significantly lower in comparison, she did not mind this change, because for her less money brought more happiness.

Besides the language barrier, there was another hurdle my parents had to overcome in an effort to prove their worth. The measuring system had them stumped, and without a doubt it developed into another one of those nasty contributors to their daily frustrations. They were proficient with meters for distance, grams and kilos for mass, and litres for liquid and volume.

Now they were expected to translate and convert all that knowledge into cups, pints, quarts and gallons for fluid; pounds and ounces for weight; and inches, feet, yards and miles for distance. Filtering through this system seemed almost absurd, and it was unbelievable to them that Canada was still using the English or the Imperial system of measurement when most other countries had moved on to metric. It took my parents, like most other immigrants, several attempts to make progress, but they eventually learned it all. Little did they know that in future years, Canada would eventually adopt the metric system. When that happened, just like many others, they had to unlearn what they had learned and relearn what they had known before in their previous life in Italy.

In addition to these barriers, Italian immigrants quite often endured injustices and discrimination because they were looked upon as people prone to violence due to their fascist background and their reputation for organized crime. They were also blamed for taking jobs away from Canadians and for producing an excessive amount of garbage. I suppose now we know where the idea of the garbage bins must have originated from.

In an effort to ease their transition, most Italians searched and found their much needed support among other fellow citizens. Eventually, this desire to belong gave rise to many *"Little Italy"* localities which were put in place with bars, clubs, pizza parlors and espresso shops.

As more and more Italians immigrated to Canada, they began to take over the construction industry and by 1960 the records show there were in excess of 10,000-13,000 Italian men employed in the construction fields of the

Toronto area alone. Even though these workers were faced with poor operational conditions, the Italian labourers' push for a support role along with their sheer persistence for renewed cultural and economical contributions actually led the way to many labour reforms.

Nostalgia and the Way Forward

Many months went by, and with a degree of nostalgia still creating misty minds, my parents had several conversations contemplating whether they should continue to adjust to the Canadian lifestyle or return to Italy, where their home sat empty and lonely, waiting for their return.

Photos of the abandoned
family property taken in 2012.

Abandoned family residence

Olive tree fields

Exterior commercial-style stone oven

Fresh water well with a drinking tub for the livestock
and a storage shed in the background.

My parents made a decision to allow themselves two years to come to terms with all these adjustments, and if things did not improve for them within that time frame, then returning back home would be a wise decision and the only sensible option available to them. But, as had happened to many immigrants who preceded us, the majority of the laments and uncertainties were nullified with time and the family opted to remain in Toronto. We earnestly continued to learn about traditions and celebrations like Thanksgiving and Halloween, among others. These occurrences were entirely new and pleasantly mysterious for us. I am happy to say that we readily and with great enthusiasm adopted the Thanksgiving national public holiday, which falls on the second Monday of October, and we learned to appreciate its symbolic meaning.

It suited us just fine to know that although this was a celebration meant for giving thanks for our good fortune during the past year, the festivity was accompanied by the indulgence in a lavish meal comprised of roasted turkey with stuffing, mashed potatoes with gravy, cranberry sauce, pumpkin pie and a variety of other foods and vegetables. Of course, for the Italians, the meal was customarily considered superb when it included a pasta dish, a few glasses of wine, espresso coffee with Sambuca (known as *caffe corretto*) and a little grappa. Let us not forget to mention the benefit of a day off work and an opportunity for cottage goers to spend the long weekend away before the winter arrived.

Halloween and the spirit of the jack-o'-lantern were also very new to us, and it took us a while to figure out why people would buy a large pumpkin, cut off the top, take out the pulp and the seeds, carve a sad or funny face on it and then put a light on the inside. We finally learned that this was a tradition aimed at warding off the spirits that roamed the earth. As Catholics, we had no issue going along with this celebration. In fact, we looked forward to it.

Then came the wonderful Christmas season. What a magnificent display of the most creative exterior decorations the Canadians exhibited! I thought that the cost of electrical energy must be very cheap in this country. These illuminations were fervently placed in large department stores and on the exterior walls and lawns of many, many homes. There was a multitude of red and green lights hanging from the roofs. Frosty the Snowman was stationed on countless lawns, and nativity sets were waiting for Christmas Eve to add baby Jesus to the cradle. We saw reindeers riding Santa's sleigh, trees decorated with glittering lights and window displays that relayed messages for the "Best of the Season" to everyone.

For us, this new tradition spoke of warmth, charm, peace, harmony and beauty. How miraculous was that?

At first, I did not understand why green and red were the dominant Christmas colours, but then I learned that they were symbolic of the Christian beliefs that green meant eternal life and red represented the blood that was shed by Jesus. Furthermore, I learned that this decorating tradition was brought to life during the 1800s by Woolworth's, a large American department store. During that time, Germany was a major producer of glass ornaments, and Woolworth's started to import such items for the purpose of adorning their stores in an effort to help lift people's spirits during this very magical period of the year.

As time went by, the concept completely caught on, and it became such a popular tradition that it quickly found its way to residential homes as well. Since we know that the nature of business has always included competitiveness, Japan wasted no time in taking the monopoly away from Germany, mass-producing glass ornaments and selling them at a reduced cost. Of course, once the Czech Republic and America realized that this was a multimillion-dollar business that brought an avalanche of happiness to the public, they too joined in the competition.

Today, decorating for Christmas has become something of a commercial affair, but it still delivers all the right qualities to a multitude of people at this special annual celebration.

Claiming My Breathing Space

By now, this cosmopolitan city called Toronto was slowly but surely becoming our permanent home. In fact, my parents ultimately applied for a mortgage, received a quick approval and went on to purchase a home and a car. Each day seemed to increase our feelings of fulfillment and of becoming settled. The next step was to apply for Canadian citizenship—and that, too, was accomplished without intimidation. A sense of belonging was swiftly emerging, and life here was becoming an open window of opportunity for us all. We developed many friendships. Financial stability provided for our comfort. Our personal safety did not seem to be threatened, the language barrier had been minimized, and my brothers and I had adapted quite well to the Canadian school system.

Years went by, and as much as my parents accepted and adapted to their new lifestyle in Toronto, they most certainly did not believe that their children should follow the Canadian tradition of joining in any sports or other extracurricular activities. When translated, the list of don'ts included no skating, no swimming and definitely no after-school participation in volleyball games. Furthermore, in our firm patriarchal family setting, it was especially unfashionable and unseemly for a girl to engage in any of those activities. Things were not looking very favourable for me, an active teenager.

So, as a young girl growing up in a very traditional environment which was not in sync with current thoughts on male/female equality, I—like many other young immigrant girls—felt robbed of the potential for economic and personal growth. My brothers, on the other hand, had my parents' blessing and their financial support if they chose to pursue higher education or a professional career. From my female perspective, this double standard was wrong, and so, I refused to blindly go along with it. But, as much as I protested, my attempts proved to be ineffective. In the face of this nail-biting situation, I abandoned all efforts at additional open dialogue and retired to my room in search of probable ways to get around this bizarre custom. My mother quietly whispered for me to obey my father's rules. Obviously, she was not exactly keen on being her daughter's life coach.

Dating was another quandary I come upon as I got older. No surprise, any argument over this matter was quashed without discussion. My parents, in their short-sightedness, did not consent to any reasonable options where I (a girl) was concerned. Without the tiniest bud of evidence or any convincing argument, they accepted as true that this practice was only appropriate for young males. I never understood that concept. After all, how could young men go on dates if the young women were denied the same right? Who could these young men actually be dating? My questions never got a reasonable or rational response. So life continued on, with nothing but questions and restrictions for me.

I longed to call this unfair model and unjust control what it really was; gender bias without justification. However, it was wiser to adapt than to fight such insurmountable odds in an effort to undo an unbreakable tradition.

A similar pattern was apparent when my interest in music started to take shape. Like many teenagers, I became a fan of, and was preoccupied by, rock bands like the Beatles and the Monkees. Their long hair manifestation and their lyrics energized most young people's musical interest and left a number of youngsters with laryngitis at the end of their concerts. I dared to set my hopes on getting a ticket for one of those concerts. I thought I should be good for at least one.

Let's just say that the sixties was a decade that started to pry open the door of female empowerment, that's when I became overjoyed to see the edge I was searching for. For most of us young European girls, the main struggle was that in general, any changes in our personal affairs would at best advance with extreme caution and most likely without resolution. No immediate light was shining in these girls' corners; there were no concert tickets either.

My father claimed it was because of their concern for my safety, but I was convinced that, contrary to their thinking, Prime Minister John Diefenbaker's vigorous leadership had already put proper safety measures in place in Canada; therefore, their caution was nothing but a ludicrous attempt to keep me sheltered and away from large and possibly rowdy crowds.

My parents even went as far as endeavour to convince me that these entertainers were nothing more than long-haired bums who generated loud noises with the help of illegal drugs. Against that strong parental attitude, my opinion did not matter a heck of a lot. Every event and each request determined who was in control, and, it definitely was not me.

To my mind, their assumptions were totally deceiving and backward, based only on the fact that any rock group's music was significantly different from their much-appreciated ballroom music. A slow Viennese waltz, a mean tango or a sophisticated quickstep always perked up their ears and tickled their feet. My father was no Fred Astaire, but he sure had all the right moves.

Suppressing many yawns and draining my last bit of hopeful energy, I eventually came to terms with the fact that there was no probable likelihood that continued arguments or my own common-sense approach would amount to anything other than a nice dream without the possibility of change. I did not possess the personal resources to bring about many, if any, significant modifications. It was my belief that a search for a solution had a strong probability of failure, but I could also gamble on the possibility of success. With that idea in mind, I took a number of disparaging chances but was never effective in resolving or winning any of the ongoing arguments.

And so, I did the only thing I knew how to do: I pursed my teenage lips, exhaled loudly and shook my head in disappointment. Through this unsettling process that seemed to be taking a snail's pace towards my emancipation,

I resolved to reconcile the two worlds I was trapped in without letting panic take over. I never considered giving up as a viable option. Whoever said "Where there is a will there is a way" was an absolute genius.

I was now about to graduate with honours from high school, and I had realized that I enjoyed and excelled in math, accounting and economics (while I could easily do without geography and gym). You can understand why my aspiration to continue my education in those favourite subjects, especially in accounting, was so meaningful for me. But it was not in my father's plans to support his daughter through higher education.

He felt that girls had a lot of other responsibilities to tend to, such as cooking, cleaning, laundry and grocery shopping, just to mention a few. Furthermore, once a girl got a husband, other family responsibilities would develop. His theory was that girls were meant to be homemakers and did not have the ability to manage a career as well. Those few females who tried to pursue one were labelled "pretentious queens." He actually believed that I would one day thank him. Not so. Instead, I opted not to partake in any more crapshoot games with my parents because I knew I would always be on the losing end. Without giving away my ideas any longer, I decided to turn this argument into a new twist in my life.

In retrospect, I really believe I made the right call.

Refusing to be disappointed, I sought full-time employment, determined to start earning a salary. It didn't take me long to land a job that paid a decent wage, enabling me to save and build the financial cushion I needed to pursue an education via correspondence or through night school. With these savings, I was now able to continue studying accounting, economics, credit and collections, and I also enjoyed a few courses in commercial law.

I was, and still am, a staunch believer that if you truly want to reach your goal, whatever that goal may be, you set your mind to turbo-boost and you find a way to make it happen. Throwing your hands up in defeat is easy, but not worthy of much. Using determination and craftiness to eliminate those intrusive roadblocks can be a daunting experience, but there is always the possibility that it will be rewarding in the end. To do nothing about a disadvantaged situation is to accelerate whatever fate has in store.

In the words of Margaret Thatcher, "Disciplining yourself to do what you know is right and important, although difficult, is the highroad to pride, self-esteem, and personal satisfaction."

On-the-Job Exploits

My first full-time job was in the credit department of a large publishing company. It was there that I gained a great deal of knowledge about advertising, collection and the significance of billing accuracy and month-end reports. I remained employed with this company for seven years, and I can honestly say that I totally enjoyed working there—with and for some fantastic people. The only disadvantage of this job was the travel time from my home. The office was quite far from my house, and given that I did not own a vehicle, my commute involved riding a bus to the nearest subway station, taking the train to a downtown intersection, transferring to another train and then walking a short distance to finally arrive at the office.

All this travelling made my eight-hour workday about twelve hours long, and some winter days even longer. But I did not take exception to it, because I enjoyed my job and looked forward to going to work every morning.

One morning, an interesting thing happened while I was on my way to catch the bus. From the corner of my eye, I noticed a green Cutlass Supreme car slowing down as it drove towards me. The lone male driver appeared to have fixed a stare on me that did not budge until I reached the bus shelter. Then he drove off. The next day, the same car followed me at every turn of the road and then sped off once I reached the bus-stop area.

On day three, this occurrence started to look less like a coincidence and more like an intentional exercise. On day four, I had no urge to chance another one of these unnecessary occurrences, so I thought I would play it safe and outsmart him by leaving the house ten minutes later, hoping that whoever this stranger was would have driven away already. But, to my surprise, as I made my way to the bus stop, I noticed the infamous green car parked just up the street. Determined to put an end to this cat-and-mouse game, I tested my courage and continued on my path past that vehicle. With an alarming feeling of uncertainty and apprehension, I quickly became aware of that relentless stare, which did not differ from the previous ones. As my feelings surged from discomfort to anger because this man was intruding into my privacy, I promptly stared back and gave him the typical Italian greeting (the finger). With that, he drove away.

A few weeks passed without any sign of that Cutlass Supreme. I believed I had taken care of the situation—or perhaps it was nothing more than a ridiculous hoax. And so I gradually let my guard down. I did not have the fuzziest notion that a more direct form of introduction was being planned.

One Friday morning, as I was making my unsuspecting way to the subway train, I was shocked to see the gentleman from the Cutlass standing there right in front of me. Being aware that confused emotions can oftentimes trigger confused results, I did my best to keep my composure as this gentleman introduced himself and, with much respect, apologized for causing me any concern as to my safety. He rode the train with me all the way downtown and then wished me a good day. I began to believe that he really was not much of a threat; rather, he was a very caring individual on a personal mission.

Each day brought more conversations, building into an increasingly open and frank dialogue. Within a few months, the authenticity of our communication developed into the base for a successful relationship. We spoke honestly about many important topics and agreed that different people have different opinions and diverse points of view. There was my truth and there was your truth. We agreed that no perspective should be shared in a threatening or overpowering manner, although quite often this can be an area requiring a lot of work and effort from both parties.

Figuring that this relationship was unexpectedly shaping up like the Boston Marathon—that is, long-running—the thought of serious dedication put a new spin on life. He spoke of "commitment," and I heard "partnership." A year later, we signed up for marriage, and we have been together ever since.

For me, this significant pronouncement did not represent an opportunity to avoid or escape from strict rules or parental control. I was simply making a new life for myself with a different beginning and a style more representative of who I really was.

This was a choice I made by myself and for myself. My thought and decision had no reason to shift off course nor did any doubt float up with regards to this new personal journey. In fact, I believe, that day nature was telling me something and I was paying attention to details.

From the beginning or our relationship, I identified many positive signs confirming we were in agreement to share a balanced division of chores, give unreserved support to one another, and, I felt confident that if children were added to our equation, he would not skip out on his responsibilities. Each of our objectives freely spoke of different benchmarks and all our conversations suggested that by dismissing the outdated structure of he/she inequality, we could create smart and efficient family economics that would produce good quality household returns. Time validated our mission.

Now, when people ask me where I met my husband, I tell them "on the street." It may sound like a cheap cliché, but it is absolutely and literally a true story.

A year and a half later, my husband and I decided to start a family. I was super excited, very ready, motivated and emotionally prepared to be a stay-at-home mom so I could nurture and love someone I knew I would care very much about. Three weeks before my daughter Sabina's arrival, I willingly made my temporary exit from the workforce to prepare my world for her appearance. Her first few years as the only child were a real success, without a doubt, and three years later my son, David, made his grand entrance into the world and joined the family. We felt so proud and complete, but my daughter said she would have preferred the quiet one in the next crib—the one wrapped in a pink blanket.

Honestly, these two young children made an everlasting mark that taught me the real meaning of family love, unconditional caring and the lengths to which a parent is willing to go to overcome any obstacle that might impair her children's welfare.

When my son was 2 years old, I contemplated incorporating some work-from-home activities into our family life—or, better still, continuing my education by way of additional correspondence business courses. I established that I could handle an arrangement that included motherhood and study. I considered myself to be a full-time mom with part-time school studies, and I was confident there was no danger of me going bananas. With my husband's support (even though he did not, and still does not, share my interest in entrepreneurship), I went ahead busying myself with the planned mission without the slightest feeling of being stifled. We initially agreed to give this arrangement two years, and it surely survived the test of time.

The growth of our family made us realize that we now had to find ways to make our dollar stretch a little further, as the financial outflow had increased and the annual income had decreased. Just like many other young couples who faced the same struggles when they took on their most significant vocation of parenthood, we too learned to manage these daily variables quite effectively. This was our time to appreciate the fundamental worth of a few dollars, and together we mastered the art of avoiding the perils of a shortfall. Not easy, but certainly doable.

I must confess, my school activities were particularly accommodating, because in his free time, my husband took over the care of the children so I could focus on my studies. When the children were napping, he was no stranger to the kitchen, and he made no fuss about helping out with the meals.

Once my son reached school age, I was ready to join the workforce again, except this time I was selective about my employment location. I was adamant about finding work that did not take me too far from my children, and I made sure my new employer was aware of my parental role and prime responsibility. My quest for a new job brought me to a distribution firm located close to my home. The management was readily willing to factor in my motherhood responsibilities.

My enthusiastic return to work meant that we had to arrange for a part-time babysitter and a responsible and trusted person to ensure our children's safety to and from school. Any parent who has been through such an experience will agree that at a time like this, your emotions are put through heart-rending tests. Fortunately for us, we had the most qualified lady for the job living right across the street. Her dedication and care for the children's well-being was second to none. Even today, she continues to show both my children commendable concern and respect, and they do the same for her.

Sharing my situation with the new employer did not diminish my motivation, nor did it affect the company's decision to offer me a position of accountability for six associate depots located across Western Canada. I reported to the vice president of finance—who was nicknamed "the angry wolf." This long-standing designation was still attached to his name eight years later when I finally moved on to a better and more civilized company.

This man was maniacally austere in his management style, but the company prospered under his rule. He instilled fear in the employees and outright denounced failure. The upside was that he taught us how to think fast on our feet and shared his accumulated operational knowledge freely and without reserve. We appreciated the height of the bar he set for his business, but we could not accept his total lack of compassion towards any employee who, in his estimation, did not measure up. Nor did he flinch when he brought someone to tears. His callous habit of bringing people's self-esteem down to zero and then chasing them out of the office became a weekly occurrence.

The revolving doors of that establishment endured some serious and antagonistic calisthenics.

Much like the others, I worked very hard and learned plenty from him during my eight-year tenure. However, the last two years of employment with that firm felt like I was in a boot camp. Consequently, one day, at the first sign of trouble, I reached the end of my rope with his insolence and, without hesitation or regret, joined my ex-colleagues in calling it quits. Now I was out of a job, but I felt much better. That boot camp for me was closed.

After two short weeks of unemployment, I was recruited by a manufacturing firm as assistant controller. This was a family-run business with its main operation in Toronto and two subsidiary locations in other Canadian cities. The president was an amazing leader who had a mind like a sponge and did not need a computer to calculate inventory or keep track of sales figures, which in his eyes were the driving force of his business. Figuring out the value of the bottom line was the accountant's responsibility. After one short year of service with this company, I was invited by the president to become involved in discussions relating to his company real estate deals, new equipment and product acquisitions, legal matters and banking negotiations. What a positively constructive training ground that position proved to be. I definitely owed this undeniably remarkable business tutor a deep debt of gratitude.

As I continued my employment with this company, I began to develop a hint of courage that seriously got me thinking about starting my own business. It would happen just as soon as I figured out what industry would be a good and sensible fit for me. I was not in a hurry, nor was I trying to beat the occupational clock. I was, however, at a point in my life where I was ready to test my potential so I dared to flick a match and tip its burning flame towards a new source of revenue.

I cannot point to the precise moment my decision to venture into entrepreneurship was made, but I can confirm that it happened the second I plunged into taking lots of notes and mused over the lessons I had learned from each and every employer I worked for. Here are some treasured lessons I soaked up and took with me as a rookie being trained by motivated and highly experienced individuals bound to teach me the way business goals are met:

- Practice teamwork, and it will bring out a sense of common purpose.
- Master the art of making quick and deliberate decisions.

- Become skilled at absorbing the shock when a decision is deemed a failure.
- Always assess the reason for failure, learn from it, and move forward at electrifying speed.
- Complacency is economically counterproductive and must be avoided.
- Never attempt to perform through someone else's accomplishments.
- Ensure your commerce booklet does not include skepticism.

Enriched by this information and backed by a bag full of hope and optimism, I took a leap of faith.

A Daunting Task

Do I like to dream? Of course I do. Just like many of you, I especially endorse it when it comes with the potential for personal growth and betterment. Let's talk about the joy of making dreams a reality. Let's also be honest with ourselves and evaluate whether we are leaders or followers or simply prefer to stand on the sidelines and observe.

In my own case, I concluded that I was and still am a realist who manoeuvres away from delusions and fantasies. In parallel with that assessment goes my guarded personality traits that did not and still do not allow me to flip-flop between honestly acquired subject knowledge and false pretensions masked as talent. Even though I had many years of practice in office administration and general business management, the possibility of a new venture would not lull me into thinking that the first healthy fiscal quarter would qualify me to crack any big leagues. I was also aware of two major factors: (1) running my own business would not be a simple Monday-to-Friday undertaking, and (2) my acquired experience did not give me the winning ticket to one day become the Goliath of any industry. In essence, my own reasoning directed me towards a rational and consistent business graph with a discipline for attainable goals.

Day after day, the idea of starting a business kept surfacing in my mind with vivid insistence. I distinctly remember the excitement I felt that cloudy Thursday morning when I settled on the direction I wanted to trudge in. Promptly, I stopped waiting for the security industry to show me a gesture of acceptance and forged ahead without a second thought.

With trembling fingers I dialled the lawyer's office number and set an appointment to see him the very next day. On Friday afternoon, the corporation's registration was set in motion. Once the significant task of self-evaluation had led me to the security industry, I knew that such a move would bring about a mother lode of gossip and plenty of nonverbal language.

My determination did not waver even when it became evident that my entrance into such a diversely regulated industry would provoke a barrage of different thoughts and deliver an unexpected whiplash to my counterparts. Notwithstanding several of those meaningless hardships, after a time, I, together with my support staff sponsored a few industry rules and revisions when and where we saw the need. Our message was simply this: Business should not and must not be a place for adversity.

Here I will refer to a book I authored in 2015 entitled *This Head of Security Wears High Heels*, in which I shared the many adversities, pressures, setbacks and quandaries that could have sabotaged my success—and the obstacles that threatened to knock me down. It was a thorny and true showdown. I also discussed a flood of positive experiences that were drawn from my decree of observation, inquisitive listening and information gathering.

You may ask: How can one defend oneself against unfair and preposterous accusations without losing one's cool? Well, when faced with questionable truths or dishonest behaviour exhibited or delivered by toxic interlopers, you are well advised to dig deep into the matter. Do not stop until you uncover the dynamics of the real truth. Many times a story is articulated with several deliberate untruths and is void of substance or merit. I know this because I have dealt with many antiventure employees who suffer from "I tell the truth my way" syndrome and as far as I can tell, medical science is still searching for an antidote to this hard-to-square disease. Straightforwardness and professional efforts combined with a margin of corporate legal defence will shelter you and your company from these unsubstantiated claims that bring with them the potential for ruin. I suspect you will agree with me that, categorically speaking, business is not the foe, though people definitely can be, and in more ways than one.

Sometimes when I wake up and prepare for the day ahead, my ears hone-in to the echo of this question: "Are female chief executive officers of a company *actual* CEOs, or are they thought of as *female* CEOs?"

Then I look at the following award, and the question is answered:

One of my very proud and precious moments.

My Pivotal Observations

Flipping through the pages of my desk calendar one day, a revelation spoke out to me in a volume that easily overpowered the loud squealing of the phone lines. This eye-opening message became a valuable learning moment for me. The memorandum claimed that life is a precious gift given to us without instructions and what we make of it is up to each one of us. We can choose to dance to the drumbeat of the uncanvassed and risk becoming a dormant society with no energy for thought or improvement. Alternatively, we can opt for self determination and strive without reservation to achieve our objectives in both our personal and professional life. To simply talk about the need to make changes is not enough to snap a disadvantage or a limitation into a pleasant accomplishment. I think I have been around long enough to observe that if we have the prerogative to change our mind, then, certainly, we must have the wherewithal to effect changes in our lives. We can select to use experiences, discoveries, understanding our true self and our goals, have the resolution to overcome any restrictions placed on us by others, and, along with the anticipation and foresight to pursue positive results, we will inch our way towards a more contented life style.

So, today, as I reflect on my bounty of childhood memories, I am grateful for life's lessons freely passed on to me by family and friends. They unreservedly and selflessly enriched my thoughts and my character all the way to adulthood. They taught me to let the light shine on whatever I do each day—and, above all, always look forward to what tomorrow might bring. Permitting myself some boldness here, I can say that regardless of our nationality or heritage, there is always someone we can look up to, admire or be inspired by. So how do we preserve this nucleus of influence while validating and adjusting to our ever-changing world? I say we embrace change.

In my dictionary, *change* encompasses different cultures, new technology, new customs and an understanding and appreciation for diverse ethnic celebrations and life. It is also of great importance to accept that one person may have an individual point of view, and society may share a similar point of view, but as individuals, we should all participate and engage in open and informative conversation with each other. This way, we will create and appreciate a culture that is enriched by realistic political and socioeconomic knowledge and impartiality.

My life has undoubtedly been influenced by many people, yet it has mostly been inspired by the strength and resolve I saw in my paternal grandmother, nonna Maria Rosa. Her life's stage was set with resilience, flexibility, eagerness and enthusiasm. She was relatable, collaborative and forthcoming, and she had a passion to live life to the fullest.

In the present day, I bear in mind the profile of this progressive woman who stood on the podium of her life. She was a silent speaker, gesturing for us to look and advance in a straightforward direction without wavering in our goals and objectives.

She spoke of resourcefulness, and we heard.

She loved to sing, and we understood her lyrics.

She believed in women's right to vote, and we all basked in that success.

She loved to tell jokes, and we laughed.

She held up a mirror, and we saw her reflection.

She believed things happen for a reason, and I second that theory.

She was a special person, and I salute her.

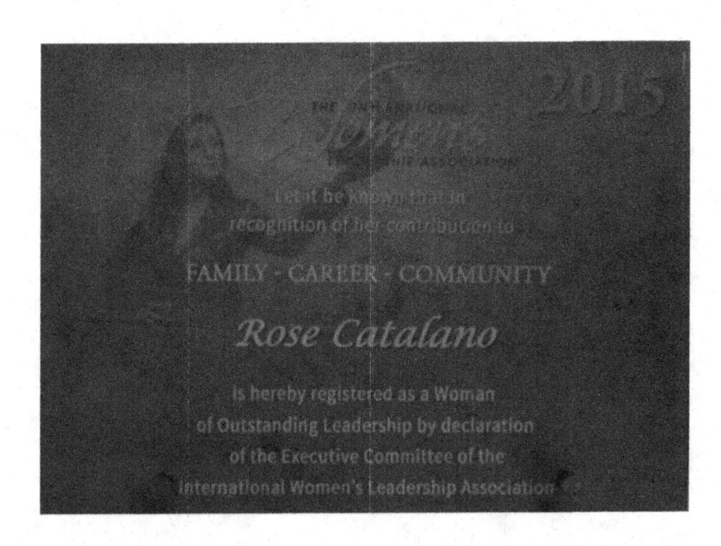

2015
Let it be known that in
recognition of her contribution to
FAMILY - CAREER - COMMUNITY
Rose Catalano
is hereby registered as a Woman
of Outstanding Leadership by declaration
of the Executive Committee of the
International Women's Leadership Association

This one is for you, nonna Maria Rosa.

Rose Catalano *is a successful businesswoman. She has been honored by the International Women's Leadership Association as a woman of outstanding leadership and is listed in the current Worldwide Who's Who Registry of Executives, Professionals and Entrepreneurs. A Child's Voyage to New Life is her second book. She currently lives with her family in Canada.*

Most of the funds from the sale of this book will be donated to the RINJ Foundation – to help and give hope to disadvantaged women and children who have been robbed of life's basic freedoms.